Evolution on Trial

Ellen Hansen, editor

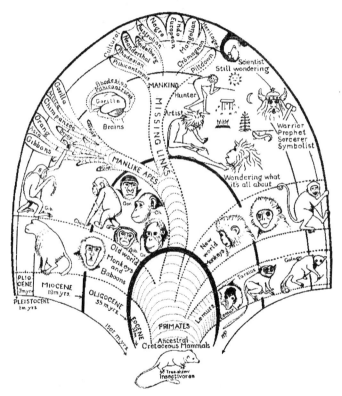

Early diagram of evolution found in a 1920's high school biology textbook.

© Discovery Enterprises, Ltd.
Lowell, Massachusetts

© Discovery Enterprises, Ltd., Lowell, MA 1994

ISBN 1-878668-34-X paperback edition
Library of Congress Catalog Card Number 94-71897

10   9   8   7   6   5   4   3   2   1

Printed in the United States of America

Subject Reference Guide:

Evolution on Trial, edited by Ellen Hansen
Scopes Trial – John T. Scopes
Evolution Verses Bible Theory of Creation
Clarence Darrow
William Jennings Bryan

Credits

Trial transcript material is excerpted from *The World's
Most Famous Court Trial: Tennessee Evolution Case*
(Ed. William Hilleary and Oren Metzger, 1925).

Photo Credits

Cover illustration and page 43 from: *Evolution - The Great
Debate*, Vernon Blackmore and Andrew Page. Oxford: Lion
Publishing, 1989; pages 19 and 39 from: *The Great Monkey
Trial: Science Versus Fundamentalism in America*, Tom
McGowen, NY: Franklin Watts, 1990.

Acknowledgments

Special thanks to Dr. Richard Cornelius, of Dayton,
Tennessee, for providing a wide range of information on the
Scopes Trial and its participants.

Dedication

*For those who listen
with an open heart,
and, therefore,
hear.*

Table of Contents

Foreword

When did life start? How old is the earth? When and how did plants, animals, and humans appear on earth?

These are important, age-old questions. Throughout history, we have tried to explain creation to ourselves. For some, religious beliefs hold the answers; for others, scientific inquiry provides the clues. These questions were also at the heart of the Scopes Trial.

The Tennessee legislature passed a law in March 1925 which effectively prohibited teaching the theory of evolution in the state's public schools and universities. The theory of evolution, as outlined by Charles Darwin in his work *The Origin of Species* (1859), proposed that the various species of plant and animal (including man) had evolved over time through the process of natural selection: survival of the fittest.

According to the creation story* in the Bible, God created the world and everything in it in six days. Many people saw the theory of evolution as a threat to their religious beliefs. They did not want their tax dollars being used to teach their children evolution in school, and worked to pass laws prohibiting such teaching.

Others were against the establishment of such laws, which they believed violated basic freedoms of teachers and students. Groups such as the American Civil Liberties Union worked to bring cases, including the Scopes case, to court to test such laws.

Both the creationists and the evolutionists felt strongly about their views. William Jennings Bryan, a famous politician and fundamentalist leader, volunteered his services to prosecute the Tennessee case against teacher John Scopes. Within days, the well-known defense attorney Clarence Darrow likewise volunteered his services, in defense of Scopes and teaching evolution. These famous participants, and the controversial issue itself, drew world-wide attention to the small Tennessee town of Dayton in the summer of 1925.

In this book, you'll explore what happened in the Scopes trial by reading primary sources--the words of people who were there. You'll also read words written later, called secondary sources, which try to interpret or explain the primary sources.

* in the text refers to notes beginning on p. 61.

The Law, the Bible, and the Case

On July 10, 1925, Judge John Raulston called on Rev. Cartwright to open court with a prayer, and the Dayton Evolution Trial (the Scopes Trial) was underway.

The first order of business was the introduction of the lawyers on both sides. For the prosecution, there was Tennessee Attorney General A.T. Stewart, William Jennings Bryan, a number of local lawyers, and Bryan's son, William Jennings Bryan, Jr. The attorneys for the defense were Clarence Darrow, Dudley Malone, Arthur Garfield Hays, and John Neal.

Judge Raulston then gave instructions to the grand jury. The duty of the grand jury was to decide whether there was enough evidence to indict* teacher John Scopes for violating Tennessee's anti-evolution statute.

Judge's Charge to the Grand Jury

The statute,* which it is alleged [John T.] Scopes violated, is Chapter 27 of the acts of 1925, ... [which] became the law in Tennessee on March 21, 1925, [and] in part reads as follows:

> Section 1. Be it enacted by the general assembly of the state of Tennessee, that it shall be unlawful for any teacher in any of the universities, normals and all other public schools

of the state, which are supported in whole or in part by the public school funds of the state, to teach any theory that denies the story of the Divine creation of man as taught in the Bible, and to teach instead that man has descended from a lower order* of animals.

Since the act involved in this investigation provides that it shall be unlawful to teach any theory that denies the divine creation of man as taught in the Bible, it is proper that I call your attention to the account of man's creation as taught in the Bible, it is proper that I call your attention to the first chapter of Genesis, reading as follows:

"In the beginning, God created the heaven and earth.
   Second--"And the earth was without form, and void; and darkness was upon the face of the deep. And the spirit of God moved upon the face of the waters.
   Third--"And God said, let there be light: and there was light.
   Fourth--"And God saw the light, that it was good: And God divided the light from the darkness.
   Fifth--"And God called the light day, and the darkness he called night. And the evening and the morning were the first day.
   Sixth--"And God said let there be a firmament in the midst of the waters, and let it divide the waters from the waters.
   Seventh--"And God made the firmament, and divided the waters which were under the firmament

from the waters which were above the firmament;
And it was so.

Eighth--"And God called the firmament heaven.
And the evening and the morning were the second
day.

Ninth--"And God said, Let the waters under the
heavens be gathered together unto one place, and
let the dry land appear, and it was so.

Ten--"And God called the dry land earth; and the
gathering together of the waters He called seas:
And God saw that it was good.

Eleventh--"And God said, let the earth bring forth
grass, the herb yielding seed, and the fruit trees
yielding fruit after his kind, whose seed is in itself,
upon the earth: And it was so.

Twelfth--"And the earth brought forth grass, and
herb yielding seed after his kind, and the tree
yielding fruit, whose seed was in itself, after his
kind; and God saw that it was good.

Thirteenth--"And the evening and the morning were
the third day.

Fourteenth--"And God said let there be lights in the
firmament of the heavens to divide the day from
the night; and let them be for signs, and for sea-
sons, and for days, and years.

Fifteenth--"And let them be for lights in the firmament of the heavens to give light upon the earth;
and it was so.

Sixteenth--"And God made two great lights: The
greater light to rule the day and the lesser light to
rule the night: He made the stars also.

Seventeenth--"And God set them in the firmament of
the heaven to give light upon the earth.

Eighteenth--"And to rule over the day and over the
night and to divide the light from the darkness:
and God saw that it was good.

Nineteenth--"and the evening, and the morning were
the fourth day.

Twentieth--"And God said, let the waters bring forth
abundantly the moving creature that hath light, and
fowls that may fly above the earth in the open firmament of heaven.

Twenty-first--"And God created great whales, and
every living creature that moveth, which the waters brought forth abundantly, after their kind, and
every winged fowl after his kind; and God saw that
it was good.

Twenty-second--"And God blessed them, saying, Be
fruitful, and multiply, and fill the waters in the
seas, and let fowl multiply in the earth.

Twenty-third--"And the evening and the morning
were the fifth day.

Twenty-fourth--"And God said, let the earth bring
forth the living creature after his kind, cattle and
creeping thing, and beasts of the earth after his
kind: And it was so.

Twenty-fifth--"And God made the beasts of the earth
after his kind, and cattle after their kind, and everything that creepeth upon the earth after his kind:
and God saw that it was good.

Twenty-sixth--"And God said, Let us make man in
our image, after our likeness: And let them have

dominion over the fish of the sea and over the fowl
of the air, and over the cattle, and over all the
earth, and over every creeping thing that creepeth
upon the earth.

Twenty-seventh--"So God created man in His own
image, in the image of God, created He him; male
and female created He them.

Twenty-eighth--"And God blessed them, and God
said unto them, be fruitful and multiply, and re-
plenish the earth, and subdue it; and have dominion over the fish of the sea and over the fowl of the
air and over every living thing that moveth upon
the earth.

Twenty-ninth--"And God said, Behold, I have given
you every herb bearing seed, which is upon the
face of all the earth and every tree, in which is the
fruit of a tree yielding seed; to you it shall be for
meat.

Thirtieth--"And to every beast of the earth, and to
every fowl of the air, and to every thing that
creepeth upon the earth, wherein there is life, I
have given every green herb for meat; and it was
so.

Thirty-first--"And God saw everything that he had
made, and behold, it was very good. And the
evening and the morning were the sixth day."

Therefore, the vital question now involved for
your consideration is, has the statute been violated by
the said John T. Scopes or any other person by teaching a theory that denies the story of the Divine Crea-

tion of man as taught in the Bible, and in Rhea County since the passage of this act and prior to this investigation.

If you find the statute has been thus violated, you should indict the guilty person or persons, as the case may be.

You will bear in mind that in this investigation you are not interested to inquire into the policy or wisdom of this legislation.

Both our state and federal governments are divided into three distinct and separate departments or branches and each has its functions and responsibilities independent of the other and there should be no interference, infringement or encroachment by the one upon the rights, duties, responsibilities and functions of the other.

The policy and wisdom of any particular legislation address itself to the legislative branch of government, provided the proposed legislation is within constitutional limitations.

Our constitution imposes upon the judicial branch the interpretation of statutes and upon the executive branch the enforcement of the law. . . .

Now, gentlemen of the jury, it is your duty to investigate this alleged offense without prejudice or bias and with open minds, and if you find that there has been a violation of the statute you should promptly return a bill,* otherwise you should return a "no bill."

The Grand Jury returned a new indictment, and Judge Raulston called for trial Case No. 5232, The State of Tennessee vs. John Thomas Scopes.

The Origin of Species

At its core, the 1925 Scopes Trial pitted science against religion: teaching the theory of evolution vs. teaching the Bible creation story in Tennessee public schools.

Almost 100 years before, in 1831, Charles Darwin had set sail on a 5-year voyage, as a naturalist aboard the H.M.S. Beagle. Darwin's collections and observations from this journey formed the foundation of his lifelong work on evolution. The following excerpt is from Darwin's best-known work, The Origin of Species (1859), *in which he explains his theory of natural selection as the mechanism for evolutionary change.*

Interestingly, Darwin had originally studied for the ministry, earning his degree at Christ's College, Cambridge, in 1831.

Can it, then, be thought improbable, seeing that variations useful to man have undoubtedly occurred, that other variations useful in some way to each being in the great and complex battle of life, should sometimes occur in the course of thousands of generations? If such do occur, can we doubt (remembering that many more individuals are born than can possibly survive) that individuals having any advantage, however slight, over the others, would have the best chance of surviving and of procreating their kind? On the other hand, we may feel sure that any variation in the least degree injurious would be rigidly destroyed.

This preservation of favourable variations and the rejection of injurious variations, I call natural selection. . . .

[Under the theory of natural selection,] all past and present organic beings can be arranged within a few great classes, in groups subordinate to groups, and with the extinct groups often falling in between the recent groups . . . The similar framework of bones in the hand of a man, wing of a bat, fin of the porpoise, and leg of the horse,--the same number of vertebrae forming the neck of the giraffe and of the elephant,-- and innumerable other such facts, at once explain themselves on the theory of descent with slow and slight successive modifications. . . .

I see no good reason why the views given in this volume should shock the religious feelings of any one. . . . A celebrated author and divine has written to me that "he has gradually learnt to see that it is just as noble a conception of the Deity to believe that He created a few original forms capable of self-development into other and needful forms, as to believe that He required a fresh act of creation to supply the voids caused by the action of His laws." . . .

But the chief cause of our natural unwillingness to admit that one species has given birth to clear and distinct species, is that we are always slow in admitting great changes of which we do not see the steps. The difficulty is the same as that felt by so many geologists, when Lyell* first insisted that long lines of inland cliffs had been formed, the great valleys excavated, by the agencies which we see still at work. The mind cannot possibly grasp the full meaning of the term of even a million years; it cannot add up and perceive the full effects of many slight variations, accumulated during an almost infinite number of generations. . . .

It is interesting to contemplate a tangled bank, clothed with many plants of many kinds, with birds singing on the bushes, with various insects flitting about, and with worms crawling through the damp earth, and to reflect that these elaborately constructed forms, so different from each other, and dependent upon each other in so complex a manner, have all been produced by laws acting around us. These laws, taken in the largest sense, being Growth with Reproduction; Inheritance which is almost implied by reproduction;* Variability from the indirect and direct action of the conditions of life, and from use and disuse: a Ratio of Increase so high as to lead to a Struggle for Life, and as a consequence to Natural Selection, entailing Divergence of Character and the Extinction of less-improved forms. Thus, from the war of nature, from famine and death, the most exalted object which we are capable of conceiving, namely the production of the higher animals, directly follows. There is grandeur in this view of life, with its several powers, having been originally breathed by the Creator into a few forms or into one; and that, whilst this planet has gone cycling on according to the fixed law of gravity, from so simple a beginning endless forms most beautiful and most wonderful have been, and are being evolved.

Center of the Storm

John Thomas Scopes was the named defendant in the Scopes Trial, yet his role in the trial itself was minimal. He was not called to testify, and spoke only once: at his sentencing.

Being in the eye of the storm, however, gave Scopes a unique view of the unfolding drama. For example, the world best remembers the battle of words between prosecution attorney William Jennings Bryan and defense attorney Clarence Darrow (see Battling Wits, *the next reading in this book). But Scopes felt that the turning point of the trial took place in arguments presented earlier by Bryan and another defense attorney--Dudley Malone.*

Scopes recounts those arguments in Center of the Storm, *the book he wrote about the trial.*

Dudley Field Malone and William Jennings Bryan had known each other for decades. Even so, no previous encounter of theirs was half as dramatic as the one at Dayton. During the early years of the Wilson administration,* Malone had served Bryan as Undersecretary of State, in reality as a go-between for Bryan and Wilson, who did not get along well together. ...

On the afternoon of Wednesday, July 15, after Judge Raulston had settled his business with the press and had ruled against our motion to quash, Malone summed up the issues for the defense ... "We will prove that whether this statute be constitutional or unconstitutional the defendant Scopes did not and could

15

not violate it. We maintain that since the defendant Scopes has been indicted under a statute which prohibits the teaching of the evolutionary theory, the prosecution must prove as part of its case what evolution is.

"So that there shall be no misunderstanding and that no one shall be able to misinterpret or misrepresent our position we wish to state at the beginning of this case the defense believes there is a direct conflict between the theory of evolution and the theories of creation as set forth in the Book of Genesis. Neither do we believe that the stories of creation as set forth in the Bible are reconcilable or scientifically correct.

"The defense will also prove by credible testimony that there is more than one theory of creation set forth in the Bible and that they are conflicting. But we shall make it perfectly clear that while this is the view of the defense we shall show by the testimony of men learned in science and theology that there are millions of people who believe in evolution and in the stories of creation as set forth in the Bible and who find no conflict between the two. The defense maintains that this is a matter of faith and interpretation which each individual must determine for himself . . .

"While the defense thinks there is a conflict between evolution and the Old Testament, we believe there is no conflict between evolution and Christianity. There may be a conflict between evolution and the peculiar ideas of Christianity which are held by Mr. Bryan as the evangelical leader of the prosecution, but we deny that the evangelical leader of the prosecution is an authorized spokesman for the Christians of the United States. The defense maintains that there is a clear distinction between God, the church, the Bible, Christianity, and Mr. Bryan. ...

"We wish to set before you evidence of this character in order to stress the importance of the theory of evolution. If the teaching of the theory of evolution in this field is to be excluded by law, you will have to find adequate training for your doctors in medical schools outside of your state or you will have to import physicians from Chicago and New York as the defendant Scopes had to import Mr. Darrow and myself."

Malone next summarized the defense's expectations. "The narrow purpose of the defense is to establish the innocence of the defendant Scopes. The broad purpose of the defense will be to prove that the Bible is a work of religious aspiration and rules of conduct which must be kept in the field of theology.

"The defense maintains that there is no more justification for imposing the conflicting views of the Bible on courses of biology than there would be for imposing the views of biologists on courses of comparative religions. We maintain that science and religion embrace two separate and distinct fields of thought and learning.

"We remember that Jesus said: 'Render unto Caesar the things that are Caesar's and unto God the things that are God's.'"

The trial proceeded. ... In the afternoon [of July 16], after the sheriff had installed ceiling fans during the noon recess, Bryan got up to argue the case against admissibility of scientific testimony. It was the moment that most of the audience had waited for. They thrilled as Bryan approached the bench. ... [B]y the time he was in the midst of his oration on scientific testimony he had the crowd eating out of his hand. He handled them so well they sat spellbound.

"The Christian believes man came from above," he said, "but the evolutionist believes he must have come from below, that is, from a lower order of animals."

It was an old stock phrase for Bryan, who made the audience laugh with him.

He showed the diagram from Hunter's *Civic Biology* to the judge. On page 194 there was a family tree and the text stated there were 518,900 animal species. He discussed these facts jocularly, eliciting laughter as he went. ... "There is that book; there is the book they were teaching your children, that man was a mammal and so indistinguishable among the mammals that they leave him there with three thousand four hundred and ninety-nine other mammals, including elephants!" Laughter and applause encouraged him. ...

"Tell me that the parents of this day have not any right to declare that children are not to be taught this doctrine? Shall not be taken down from the high plane upon which God put man? Shall be detached from the throne of God and be compelled to link their ancestors with the jungle? Tell that to these children! Why, my friend, if they believe it, they go back to scoff at the religion of their parents! And the parents have a right to say that no teacher paid by their money shall rob their children of faith in God and send them back to their homes skeptical, infidels, or agnostics, or atheists!"

Bryan stopped to read from Darwin's *Origin of Species.* He denounced a view of life without God. ... Then Bryan concluded: "The facts are simple, the case is plain, and if these gentlemen want to enter upon a larger field of educational work on the subject of evolution, let us get through with this case and then convene a mock court, or it will deserve the title of mock court if its purpose is to banish from the hearts of the people the Word of God as revealed."

As he finished there was prolonged applause, which Judge Raulston made no attempt to prevent,

Students of John Scopes were sworn in. They testified that their teacher had, indeed, taught them about the theory of evolution, which was not allowed by Tennessee law.

and it seemed that the Silver-Tongued Orator had won the day. ...

Malone, defying the stifling July heat, was the only one of us who remained fully clothed. Everyone in the court had been impressed by this fact; no one had ever seen him with his coat off, and now as he rose to answer Bryan he performed the most effective act anyone could have thought of to get the audience's undivided attention: He took off his coat. He folded it neatly and laid it carefully on the counsel's table. Every eye was upon him before he had said a single word.

He faced the bench. Instead of standing to begin his speech he half-sat on the defense table. His was the posture of a whipped creature, against whom everything in life had gone wrong. His face and his shoulders seemed to say, I'm whipped; the temperature has beaten me; my former boss has let me down; what more can happen?

"If the court please," he began, "it does seem to me that we have gone far afield in this discussion. However, probably this is the time to discuss everything that bears on the issues that have been raised in this case, because, after all, whether Mr. Bryan knows it or not, he is a mammal, he is an animal, and he is a man.
. . .

"I have been puzzled and interested at one and the same time at the psychology of the prosecution, and I find it hard to distinguish between Mr. Bryan the lawyer in this case, Mr. Bryan the propagandist outside of this case, and Mr. Bryan who made a speech against science and for religion just now, and Mr. Bryan my old chief and friend. . . . I know Mr. Bryan. I don't know Mr. Bryan as well as Mr. Bryan knows Mr. Bryan, but I know this, that he does believe, and Mr. Bryan, Your Honor, is not the only one who believes; he is not the only one who believes in God; he is not the only one who believes in the Bible."

And beginning with those words, Malone took the crowd away from Bryan the Invincible, even though Bryan had wrapped up the audience and marked it his. Soon the spectators were cheering Malone. It was so dramatic that a transcript couldn't tell it. The words themselves were not exceptional, just as Bryan's were not; it was the way Malone spoke them. . . .

As Malone pleaded on, his argument blotted out what Bryan had said. "Are we to have our children know nothing about science except what the church says they shall know? I have never seen harm in learning and understanding, in humility and open-mindedness, and I have never seen clearer the need of that learning than when I see the attitude of the prosecution, who attack and refuse to accept the information and intelligence which expert witnesses will give them.

"The difference between the theological mind and the scientific mind is that the theological mind is closed, because that is what is revealed and is settled. But the scientist says, 'No, the Bible is the book of revealed religion, with rules of conduct and with aspirations--that is the Bible.' The scientists say, 'Take the Bible as guide, as an inspiration, as a set of philosophies and preachments in the world of theology.'

"And what does this law do? We have been told here that this was not a religious question. I defy anybody, after Mr. Bryan's speech, to believe that this was not a religious question. . . .

'[W]e say: Keep your Bible. Keep it as your consolation, keep it as your guide, but keep it where it belongs, in the world of your own conscience, in the world of your individual judgment, in the world of the Protestant conscience that I heard so much about when I was a boy. Keep your Bible in the world of theology where it belongs, and do not try to tell an intelligent world and the intelligence of this country that these books written by men who knew none of the accepted fundamental facts of science, can be put into a course of science, because what are they doing here?" . . .

"I feel that the prosecution here is filled with a needless fear. I believe that if they withdrew their objection and heard the evidence of our experts, their minds would not only be improved, but their souls would be purified. . . .

"The least that this generation can do, Your Honor, is to give the next generation all the facts, all the available data, all the theories, all the information that learning, that study, that observation has produced; give it to the children in the hope to heaven that they will make a better world of this than we have been able to make of it. . . .

"We are ready to tell the truth as we understand it and we do not fear all the truth that they can present as facts. We are ready. We are ready. We feel we

stand with progress. We feel we stand with science.
We feel we stand with intelligence. We feel we stand
with fundamental freedom in America. We are not
afraid. Where is the fear? We meet it. Where is the
fear? We defy it! We ask your Honor to admit the
evidence as a matter of correct law, as a matter of
sound procedure, and as a matter of justice to the defense in this case."

The courtroom went wild when Malone finished.
The heavy applause he had received during the speech
was nothing compared to the crowd's reaction now at
the end. The judge futilely called for order. ...
Stewart followed Malone with the State's final plea
against admitting expert witnesses and although he
managed to drag in Darrow's agnosticism, there was
no hope of having court any more that day. Malone's
speech had left an electricity in the air and anything
that followed was sure to be anticlimactic; Raulston
adjourned court until the following morning, which
was Friday.

Several minutes later, the courtroom was cleared
and only three persons remained: Bryan, Malone,
and I. Bryan was sitting alone in his rocking chair by
the prosecution's table. As he tried to cool himself,
he would let the palm-leaf fan drop and then he would
stare at a spot in front of him. I was sitting with Malone at the counsel table.

Bryan, without turning, said, "Dudley, that was the
greatest speech I have ever heard!"

"Thank you, Mr. Bryan, " said Malone quietly. "I
am sorry it was I who had to make it."

Battling Wits

It was the afternoon of July 20, 1925, the seventh day of the Scopes Trial. Due to the heat and an overcrowded courtroom, the judge had moved the proceedings outside into the courtyard.

The defense attorneys called William Jennings Bryan to the stand as an expert witness on the Bible. Bryan's fellow prosecution attorneys objected, saying that the defense shouldn't be calling a prosecution attorney to testify on the witness stand. But Bryan agreed to testify, setting the stage for the most dramatic exchange of the trial.

Mr. Hays--The defense desires to call Mr. Bryan as a witness, and, of course, the only question here is whether Mr. Scopes taught what these children said he taught, we recognize what Mr. Bryan says as a witness would not be very valuable. We think there are other questions involved, and we should want to take Mr. Bryan's testimony for the purposes of our record, even if your honor thinks it is not admissible in general, so we wish to call him now. . . .

The Court--Mr. Bryan, you are not objecting to going on the stand?

Mr. Bryan-- Not at all.

The Court--Do you want Mr. Bryan sworn?

Mr. Darrow--No.

Mr. Bryan--I can make affirmation; I can say "So help me God, I will tell the truth."

Mr. Darrow--No, I take it you will tell the truth, Mr. Bryan.

Examination of W. J. Bryan by Clarence Darrow, of counsel for the defense:

Q--You have given considerable study to the Bible, haven't you, Mr. Bryan?

A--Yes, sir, I have tried to.

Q--Well, we all know you have, we are not going to dispute that at all. But you have written and published articles almost weekly, and sometimes have made interpretations of various things?

A--I would not say interpretations, Mr. Darrow, but comments on the lesson.

Q--If you comment to any extent these comments have been interpretations.

A--I presume that my discussion might be to some extent interpretations, but they have not been primarily intended as interpretations.

Q--But you have studied that question, of course?

A--Of what?

Q--Interpretation of the Bible.

A--On this particular question?

Q--Yes, sir.

A--Yes, sir.

Q--Then you have made a general study of it?

A--Yes, I have; I have studied the Bible for about fifty years, or sometime more than that, but, of course, I have studied it more as I have become older than when I was but a boy.

Q--Do you claim that everything in the Bible should be literally interpreted?

A--I believe everything in the Bible should be accepted as it is given there; some of the Bible is given illustratively. For instance: "Ye are the salt of the earth." I would not insist that man was actually salt, or that he had flesh of salt, but it is used in the sense of salt as saving God's people. . . ,

Q--The Bible says Joshua commanded the sun to stand still for the purpose of lengthening the day, doesn't it, and you believe it?

A--I do.

Q--Do you believe at that time the entire sun went around the earth?

A--No, I believe that the earth goes around the sun.

Q--Do you believe that the men who wrote it thought that the day could be lengthened or that the sun could be stopped?

A--I don't know what they thought.

Q--You don't know?

A--I think they wrote the fact without expressing their own thoughts. . . .

Q--Don't you believe that in order to lengthen the day it would have been construed that the earth stood still?

A--I would not attempt to say what would have been necessary, but I know this, that I can take a glass of water that would fall to the ground without the strength of my hand and to the extent of the glass of water I can overcome the law of gravitation and lift it up. Whereas without my hand it would fall to the ground. If my puny hand can overcome the law of gravitation, the most universally understood, to that extent, I would not set power to the hand of Almighty God that made the universe.

Mr. Darrow--I read that years ago. Can you answer my question directly? If the day was lengthened by stopping either the earth or the sun, it must have been the earth?

A--Well, I should say so.

Q--Yes? But it was language that was understood at that time, and we now know that the sun stood still as it was with the earth.

Q--We know also the sun does not stand still?

A--Well, it is relatively so, as Mr. Einstein would say.

Q--I ask you if it does stand still?

A--You know as well as I know.

Q--Better. You have no doubt about it?

A--No. And the earth moves around.

Q--Yes?

A--But I think there is nothing improper if you will protect the Lord against your criticism.

Q--I suppose He needs it?

A--He was using language at that time the people understood.

Q--And that you call "interpretation?"

A--No, sir; I would not call it interpretation.

Q--I say, you would call it interpretation at this time, to say it meant something then?

A--You may use your own language to describe what I have to say, and I will use mine in answering.

Q--Now, Mr. Bryan, have you ever pondered what would have happened to the earth if it had stood still?

A--No.

Q--You have not?

A--No; the God I believe in could have taken care of that, Mr. Darrow.

Q--I see. Have you ever pondered what would naturally happen to the earth if it stood still suddenly?

A--No.

Q--Don't you know it would have been converted into a molten mass of matter?

A--You testify to that when you get on the stand, I will give you a chance.

Q--Don't you believe it?

A--I would want to hear expert testimony on that.

Q--You have never investigated that subject?

A--I don't think I have ever had the question asked.

Q--Or ever thought of it?

A--I have been too busy on things that I thought were of more importance than that.

Q--You believe the story of the flood to be a literal interpretation?

A--Yes, sir.

Q--When was that flood?

A--I would not attempt to fix the date. The date is fixed, as suggested this morning.

Q--About 4004 B.C.?

A--That has been the estimate of a man that is accepted today. I would not say it is accurate.

Q--That estimate is printed in the Bible?

A--Everybody knows, at least, I think most of the people know, that was the estimate given.

Q--But what do you think that the Bible, itself, says? Don't you know how it was arrived at?

A--I never made a calculation.

Q--A calculation from what?

A--I could not say.

Q--From the generations of man?

A--I would not want to say that.

Q--What do you think?

A--I do not think about things I don't think about.

Q--Do you think about things you do think about?

A--Well, sometimes.

(Laughter in the courtyard.)

The Policeman--Let us have order. . . .

Mr. Darrow--How long ago was the flood, Mr. Bryan?
. . .

The Witness--It is given here, as 2348 years B.C.

Q--Well, 2348 B.C. You believe that all the living things that were not contained in the ark were destroyed.

A--I think the fish may have lived.

Q-- Outside of the fish?

A--I cannot say.

Q--You cannot say?

A--No, except that just as it is, I have no proof to the contrary.

Q--I am asking you whether you believe?

A--I do.

Q--That all living things outside of the fish were destroyed.

A--What I say about the fish is merely a matter of humor. . . .

Q--Let us make it definite, 2348 years?

A--I didn't say that. That is the time given there

(indicating a Bible) but I don't pretend to say that is exact.

Q--You never figured it out, these generations, yourself?

A--No sir; not myself.

Q--But the Bible you have offered in evidence, says 2340 something, so that 4200 years ago there was not a living thing on the earth, excepting the people on the ark and the animals of the ark and the fishes?

A--There have been living things before that.

Q--I mean at that time?

A--After that.

Q--Don't you know there are any number of civilizations that are traced back to more than 5,000 years?

A--I know we have people who trace things back according to the number of ciphers they have. But I am not satisfied they are accurate.

Q--You are not satisfied there is any civilization that can be traced back 5,000 years?

A--I would not want to say there is because I have no evidence of it that is satisfactory. ...

Q--You believe that all the various human races on the earth have come into being in the last 4,000 years or 4,200 years, whatever it is?

A--No, it would be more than that. ...

Q--Let me make this definite. You believe that every civilization on the earth and every living thing, except possibly the fishes, that came out of the ark were wiped out by the flood?

A--At that time.

Q--At that time. And then, whatever human beings, including all the tribes, that inhabited the world, and have inhabited the world, and who run their pedigree straight back, and all the animals, have come onto the earth since the flood?

A--Yes.

Q--Within 4,200 years. Do you know a scientific man on the face of the earth that believes any such thing?

A--I cannot say, but I know some scientific men who dispute entirely the antiquity of man as testified to by other scientific men. ...

Q--Don't you know that the ancient civilizations of China are 6,000 or 7,000 years old, at the very least?

A--No; but they would not run back beyond the creation, according to the Bible, 6,000 years.

Q-- You don't know how old they are, is that right?

A-- I don't know how old they are, but probably you do. (Laughter in the courtyard.) I think you would give the preference to anybody who opposed the Bible, and I give the preference to the Bible.

Q--I see. Well, you are welcome to your opinion. Have you any idea how old the Egyptian civilization is?

A--No. ... I have all the information I want to live by and to die by.

Q--And that's all you are interested in?

A--I am not looking for any more on religion.

Q--You don't care how old the earth is, how old man

is and how long the animals have been here?

A--I am not much interested in that.

Q--You have never made any investigation to find out?

A--No, sir, I have never. . . .

Q--Have you any idea how old the earth is?

A--No.

Q--The book you have introduced in evidence tells you, doesn't it?

A--I don't think it does, Mr. Darrow.

Q--Let's see whether it does; is this the one?

A--That is the one, I think.

Q--It says B.C. 4004?

A--That is Bishop Usher's calculation.

Q--That is printed in the Bible you introduced?

A--Yes, sir.

Q--And numerous other Bibles?

A--Yes, sir. . . .

Q--Would you say that the earth was only 4,000 years old?

A--Oh, no; I think it is much older than that.

Q--How much?

A--I couldn't say.

Q--Do you say whether the Bible itself says it is older than that?

A--I don't think the Bible says itself whether it is older or not.

Q--Do you think the earth was made in six days?

A--Not six days of twenty-four hours.

Q--Doesn't it say so?

A--No, sir.

Gen. Stewart--I want to interpose another objection. What is the purpose of this examination?

Mr. Bryan--The purpose is to cast ridicule on everybody who believes in the Bible, and I am perfectly willing that the world shall know that these gentlemen have no other purpose than ridiculing every Christian who believes in the Bible.

Mr. Darrow--We have the purpose of preventing bigots and ignoramuses from controlling the education of the United States and you know it, and that is all.

Mr. Bryan--I am glad to bring out that statement. I want the world to know that this evidence is not for the view Mr. Darrow and his associates have filed affidavits here stating, the purposes of which I understand it, is to show that the Bible story is not true. . . .

Mr. Malone--Your honor on this very subject, I would like to say that I would have asked Mr. Bryan--and I consider myself as good a Christian as he is-- every question that Mr. Darrow has asked him for the purpose of bringing out whether or not there is to be taken in this court only a literal interpretation of the Bible, or whether, obviously, as these questions indicate, if a general and literal construction cannot be put upon the parts of the Bible which have been covered by Mr. Darrow's questions. I hope for the last time no further attempt will be made by counsel on the other side of the case, or Mr. Bryan, to say the defense is concerned at all with Mr. Darrow's particular religious views or

lack of religious views. We are here as lawyers
with the same right to our views. I have the same
right to mine as a Christian as Mr. Bryan has to
his, and we do not intend to have this case charged
by Mr. Darrow's agnosticism or Mr. Bryan's brand
of Christianity. (A great applause.)

The Court--I will pass on each question as asked, if it
is objected to.

Mr. Darrow--Mr. Bryan, do you believe that the first
woman was Eve?

A--Yes.

Q--Do you believe she was literally made out of
Adam's rib?

A--I do.

Q--Did you ever discover where Cain got his wife?

A--No sir; I leave the agnostics to hunt for her.

Q--You have never found out?

A--I have never tried to find.

Q--You have never tried to find?

A--No.

Q--The Bible says he got one, doesn't it? Were there
other people on the earth at that time?

A--I cannot say.

Q--You cannot say. Did that ever enter your consideration?

A--Never bothered me.

Q--There were no others recorded, but Cain got a
wife.

A--That is what the Bible says.

Q--Where she came from you do not know. All right.
Does the statement, "The morning and the evening

were the first day," and "The morning and the evening were the second day," mean anything to you?

A--I do not think it necessarily means a twenty-four-hour day.

Q--You do not?

A--No.

Q--What do you consider it to be?

A--I have not attempted to explain it. If you will take the second chapter--let me have the book. (Examining Bible.) The fourth verse of the second chapter says: "These are the generations of the heavens and of the earth, when they were created in the day that the Lord God made the earth and the heavens," the word "day" there in the very next chapter is used to describe a period. I do not see that there is any necessity for construing the words, "the evening and the morning," as meaning necessarily a twenty-four-hour day, "in the day when the Lord made the heaven and the earth."

Q--Then, when the Bible said, for instance, "and God called the firmament heaven. And the evening and the morning were the second day," that does not necessarily mean twenty-four hours?

A--I do not think it necessarily does.

Q--Do you think it does or does not?

A--I know a great many think so.

Q--What do you think?

A--I do not think it does.

Q--You think those were not literal days?

A--I do not think they were twenty-four-hour days.

Q--What do you think about it?

A--That is my opinion--I do not know that my opinion is better on that subject than those who think it does.

Q--You do not think that?

A--No. But I think it would be just as easy for the kind of God we believe in to make the earth in six days as in six years or in 6,000,000 years or in 600,000,000 years. I do not think it important whether we believe one or the other.

Q--Do you think those were literal days?

A--My impression is they were periods, but I would not attempt to argue as against anybody who wanted to believe in literal days.

Q--Have you any idea of the length of the periods?

A--No; I don't.

Q--Do you think the sun was made on the fourth day?

A--Yes.

Q--And they had evening and morning without the sun?

A--I am simply saying it is a period.

Q--They had evening and morning for four periods without the sun, do you think?

A--I believe in creation as there told, and if I am not able to explain it I will accept it. Then you can explain it to suit yourself. ...

Q--Now, if you call those periods, they may have been a very long time.

A--They might have been.

Q--The creation might have been going on for a very long time?

A--It might have continued for millions of years.

William Jennings Bryan

Many newspaper accounts of the Scopes Trial ridiculed William Jennings Bryan--as rigid, unthinking, almost comic in his conservatism--based on his performance as a witness in the case. Others felt he'd betrayed his fellow fundamentalists, by allowing that the "days" of creation in the Bible could just as easily refer to "periods."

Five days after trial's end, Bryan died suddenly in his sleep. Friend and foe alike then took a longer view of Bryan's life, and rediscovered his many contributions. They remembered him as a 3-time Presidential nominee, a tireless spokesperson for progressive causes from women's suffrage to world peace, and, above all, as an outstanding orator.

Bryan's last court speech in the Scopes Trial gives a glimpse of these qualities.

Mr. Bryan--I don't know that there is any special reason why I should add to what has been said, and yet the subject has been presented from so many viewpoints that I hope the court will pardon me if I mention a viewpoint that has not been referred to. Dayton is the center and the seat of this trial largely by circumstance. We are told that more words have been sent across the ocean by cable to Europe and Australia about this trial than has ever been sent by cable in regard to anything else happening in the United States. That isn't because the trial is held in Dayton. It isn't because a school-teacher has been subjected to the danger of a fine from $100.00 to $500.00, but I think illustrates how people can be drawn into prominence by attaching themselves to a great cause. Causes stir the world. It is because it goes deep. It is because it extends wide, and because it reaches into the future beyond the power of man to see. Here has been fought out a little case of little consequence as a case, but the world is interested because it raises an issue, and that issue will some day be settled right, whether it is settled on our side or the other side. It is going to be settled right. There can be no settlement of a great cause without discussion, and people will not discuss a cause until their attention is drawn to it, and the value of this trial is not in any incident of the trial, it is not because of anybody who is attached to it, either in an official way or as counsel on either side. Human beings are mighty small, your honor. We are apt to magnify the personal element and we sometimes become inflated with our importance, but the world little cares for man as an individual. He is born, he works, he dies, but causes go on forever, and we who participated in this case may congratulate ourselves that we have attached ourselves to a mighty issue. Now, if I were to attempt to define that issue, I might find objection from the other side. Their definition of the issue might not be as mine is, and therefore, I will not take advantage of the privilege the court gives me this morning to make a statement that might be controverted, and nothing that I would say would determine it. I have no power to define this issue finally and authoritatively. None of the counsel on our side has this power and none of the counsel on the other side has this power, even this honorable court has no such power. The people will determine this issue. They will take sides upon this issue, they will state the question involved in this issue, they will examine the information--not so much that which has been brought out here, for very little has been brought out here, but this case will stimulate investigation and investigation will bring out information, and the facts will be known, and upon the facts, as ascertained, the decision will be rendered, and I think, my friends, and your honor, that if we are actuated by the spirit that should actuate every one of us, no matter what our views may be, we ought not only desire, but pray, that that which is right will prevail, whether it be our way or somebody else's. (Applause.)

Bryan (with fan) chats with Darrow during a recess in the trial.

Beyond Dayton

The Scopes Trial was certainly the most colorful battle between evolutionist and creationist views. The clash between Clarence Darrow and William Jennings Bryan over questions of science, religion, and morality captured the country's attention. But it did not settle the issue.

On July 21, 1925, the eighth and final day of the Scopes Trial, Judge Raulston ruled that all expert testimony on science and religion (including Mr. Bryan's testimony on the Bible) would not be allowed in as evidence. Therefore, the jury was left with this narrow issue to decide: had John Scopes, in fact, taught that man descended from a lower order of animals, in violation of the state's anti-evolution statute? No one disagreed on that point; even the defense requested the court to instruct the jury that the defendant was guilty under the law. Within nine minutes, the jury returned with a guilty verdict, and the court fined Scopes $100.

Who won? The prosecution got what they wanted: the court had enforced the state's anti-evolution statute. The defense also got what they wanted: the right to appeal to a higher court, to test the constitutionality of that statute.

Two years later, on January 15, 1927, the Tennessee Supreme Court declared that the anti-evolution law was valid and constitutional. But the court overturned Scopes' conviction on a technicality--that the jury, not the judge, should have set the fine. This prevented an appeal of the case to the U.S. Supreme Court.

To this day, school boards, state legislatures, and courts have continued to wrestle with the issues originally raised in that Dayton courtroom in 1925. Do anti-evolution laws violate the First Amendment of the U.S. Constitution? Should both evolution and Biblical creation be taught in school? What roles should government and parents play in education, and what are the rights of teachers and students?

Through the end of the 1920s, anti-evolution bills were introduced into more than thirty state legislatures, and passed in three (Mississippi, Arkansas, and Texas). Creationists at this time also persuaded textbook publishers to downplay the evolution theory--to rewrite whole sections, or at least to delete words such as *evolution* and *Darwin* from their indexes. The debate over teaching evolution died down, and the evolutionists and creationists slid into a 30-year truce.

Then the Soviet Union launched Sputnik, the world's first manmade satellite. The year was 1957. Americans were stunned, and a bit embarrassed that the Russians had beat them to it. A surge of interest in science resulted, and this meant, among other things, more government money to update the teaching of science in schools. The Biological Sciences Curriculum Study, involving both scientists and teachers, reintroduced the theory of evolution as a major theme in the texts they produced. A majority of U.S. schools used these textbooks over the next years.

Once again, groups began forming on either side of the evolution issue, with the schools as the battleground. Two creationists wrote a book in 1961, called *The Genesis Flood*, which presented scientific evidence for the belief that the world was created as described in the Bible. Instead of relying on religious arguments, the creationists were turning to science to prove their point, and became known as scientific creationists.

But in the early 1960s, the U.S. Supreme Court was busy maintaining a "wall of separation" between religion and government in the cases it decided. Relying on the First and Fourteenth Amendments* to the U.S. Constitution, the Court in one case stopped the practice of reading Bible verses and the Lord's Prayer in public school classrooms, and in another case ruled that state-sponsored prayer in school was illegal.

Toward the end of the decade, Tennessee's legislature repealed that state's anti-evolution statute (1967) and the U.S. Supreme Court declared the Arkansas anti-evolution law unconstitutional (1968).

The scientific creationists took a new approach in the 1970s. They no longer tried to keep evolution out of the schools, but rather pushed for teaching the creation theory alongside evolution in the schools. Tennessee's "equal time" statute was passed in 1973, only to be found unconstitutional by a federal court two years later.

The creationists continued introducing such statutes into the legislatures of more than twenty other states. In the early 1980s, a "Balanced Treatment of

Montage of newspaper articles and photos from Evolution - The Great Debate.

Creation Science and Evolution Science" Act was passed in the states of Arkansas and Louisiana. Both laws were tested in federal courts, and found invalid; they violated the freedom-of-religion guarantee of the First Amendment to the U.S. Constitution. You can read part of the federal court's decision in the Arkansas case, known as "The Scopes II Trial," in this book.

On June 19, 1987, the U.S. Supreme Court ruled in the Louisiana case that scientific creationism was not science, but rather religion, and as such, could not be taught in U.S. public school classrooms. The evolutionists had won in our nation's highest court: evolution would be taught in U.S. schools, creationism would not.

Was the Louisiana case the final battle, or is this a continuing conflict? Look in your own classroom, school, and state. What do you think?

In the Beginning

Isaac Asimov (1920-1992) wrote almost 500 books in his lifetime, becoming one of the most well-known scientific writers of our time. He was already famous for his science fiction when, in 1958, he turned his attention to writing books on popular science and textbooks. The following reading is from his book In the Beginning: Science Faces God in the Book of Genesis (1981).

"In the beginning God created the heaven and the earth." The very first phrase in the Bible states that there was a beginning to things.

Why not? It seems natural. Those objects with which we are familiar have a beginning. You and I were born, and before that we did not exist, at least not in our present form. The same is true of other human beings, of plants and animals and, in fact, of all living things, as far as we know from common observation.

We are surrounded, moreover, by all the works of humanity, and all these were, in one way or another, fashioned by human beings; before that, they did not exist, at least in their fashioned form.

It seems natural to feel that if all things alive and human-fashioned had a beginning, then the rule might be universal, and that things that are neither alive nor human-fashioned might also have had a beginning.

At any rate, primitive attempts to explain the Universe start with an explanation of its beginning. This seems so natural a thing that it is doubtful if anyone ever questioned the concept of a beginning in early times, however much disagreement there may have been over the details.

And in the scientific view, there is also considered to be a beginning, not only for Earth, but for the entire Universe.

Since the Bible and science both state that heaven and earth had a beginning, does this represent a point of agreement between them?

Yes, of course--but it is a trivial agreement. There is an enormous difference between the Biblical statement of beginning and the scientific statement of beginning, which I will explain because it illuminates all subsequent agreements between the Biblical and scientific point of view; and, for that matter, all subsequent disagreements.

Biblical statements rest on authority. If they are accepted as the inspired word of God, all argument ends there. There is no room for disagreement. The statement is final and absolute for all time.

A scientist, on the other hand, is committed to accepting nothing that is not backed by acceptable evidence. Even if the matter in question seems obviously certain on the face of it, it is all the better if it is backed by such evidence.

Acceptable evidence is that which can be observed and measured in such a way that subjective opinion is minimized. In other words, different people repeating the observations and measurements with different instruments at different times and in different places should come to the same conclusion. Furthermore, the deductions made from the observations and measurements must follow certain accepted rules of logic and reason.

Such evidence is "scientific evidence," and ideally, scientific evidence is "compelling." That is, people who study the observations and measurements, and the deductions made therefrom, feel compelled to agree with the conclusions even if, in the beginning, they felt strong doubts in the matter.

One may argue, of course, that scientific reasoning is not the only path to truth; that there are inner revelations, or intuitive grasps, or blinding insights, or overwhelming authority that all reach the truth more firmly and more surely than scientific evidence does.

That may be so, but none of these alternate paths to truth is compelling. Whatever one's internal certainty, it remains difficult to transfer that certainty simply by saying, "But I'm *sure* of it." Other people very often remain unsure and skeptical.

Whatever the authority of the Bible, there has never been a time in history when more than a minority of the human species has accepted that authority. And even among those who accepted the authority, differences in interpretation have been many and violent, and on every possible point, no one interpretation has ever won out over all others.

So intense have been the differences and so unable has any one group been to impress other groups with its version of the "truth" that force has very often been resorted to. There is no need here to go into the history of Europe's wars of religion or of the burning of heretics, to give examples.

Science, too, has seen its share of arguments, disputes, and polemics; scientists are human, and scientific ideals (like all other ideals) are rarely approached in practice. An extraordinary number of such arguments, disputes, and polemics have been settled on one side or the other, and the general scientific opinion has then swung to that side because of *compelling* evidence.

And yet, no matter how compelling the evidence, it remains true, in science, that more and better evidence may turn up, that hidden errors and false assumptions may be uncovered, that an unexpected incompleteness may make itself visible, and that yesterday's "firm" conclusion may suddenly twist and change into a deeper and better conclusion.

It follows, then, that the Biblical statement that earth and heaven had a beginning is authoritative and absolute, but not compelling; while the scientific statement that earth and heaven had a beginning is compelling, but not authoritative and absolute. There is a disagreement there that is deeper and more important than the superficial agreement of the words themselves.

And even the superficial agreement of the words themselves disappears as soon as we ask a further question.

For instance, if we grant the existence of a beginning, suppose we ask just *when* that beginning took place.

The Bible does not tell us when, directly. Indeed, the Bible does not date a single event in any of the books of the King James Version in any way that would help us tie those events into a specific time in the system of chronology we use.

Nevertheless, the question of when the Creation took place has aroused curiosity, and various Biblical scholars have made every effort to deduce its date by using various statements found in the Bible as indirect evidence.

They did not come to precisely the same answer. The generally accepted conclusion among Jewish scholars, for instance, was that the date of the Creation was October 7, 3761 B.C.

James Ussher, the Anglican archbishop of Armagh, Ireland, decided in 1654, on the other hand, that the Creation took place at 9 A.M. on October 23, 4004 B.C. (Ussher's calculations for this and for the dating of other events in the Bible are usually found in all the page headings of the King James Bible.) Other calculations put the Creation as far back as 5509 B.C.

Thus, the usual estimates for the age of the heaven and earth from Biblical data run from about fifty-seven hundred to seventy-five hundred years. It is over this point that the Biblical conclusions represent an enormous disagreement with the conclusions of science.

The weight of scientific evidence is that Earth, and the solar system generally, came into being in approximately their present form about 4.6 billion years ago. The Universe, generally, came into being, it would seem, about fifteen billion years ago.

The age of Earth, then, according to science, is about six hundred thousand times the age according to the Bible, and the age of the Universe, according to science, is at least two million times the age according to the Bible. ...

[T]he scientific view sees the Universe as following its own rules blindly, without either interference or direction.

That still leaves it possible that God created the Universe to begin with and designed the laws of nature that govern its behavior. From this standpoint, the Universe might be viewed as a wind-up toy, which God has wound up once and for all and which is now winding down and working itself out in all its intricacy without having to be touched at all.

If so, that reduces God's involvement to a minimum and makes one wonder if he is needed at all. . .

There, then, is perhaps the most fundamental disagreement between the Bible and science. The Bible describes a Universe created by God, maintained by him, and intimately and constantly directed by him, while science describes a Universe in which it is not necessary to postulate the existence of God at all.

This is *not* to say, by the way, that scientists are all atheists or that any of them must be atheists of necessity. There are many scientists who are as firmly religious as any nonscientist. Nevertheless, such scientists, if they are competent professionals, must operate on two levels. Whatever their faith in God in ordinary life, they must leave God out of account while engaged in their scientific observations. They can never explain a particular puzzling phenomenon by claiming it to be the result of God's suspension of natural law.

The Scopes II Trial

A law was passed in 1981 in Arkansas requiring the teaching of scientific creationism as well as evolution. The court case brought to test the law reminded many people of the 1925 Dayton trial, earning it the nickname "The Scopes II Trial."

A significant difference between the two trials was that this time, the expert testimony of scientists and religious leaders was allowed in as evidence. The reading which follows is from the federal court's decision in the Arkansas case.

Memorandum Opinion

On March 1, 1981, the Governor of Arkansas signed into law Act 590 of 1981, entitled the "Balanced Treatment for Creation-Science and Evolution-Science Act." . . . Its essential mandate is stated in its first sentence: "Public schools within this State shall give balanced treatment to creation-science and to evolution-science." On May 27, 1981, this suit was filed challenging the constitutional validity of Act 590 on three distinct grounds.

First, it is contended that Act 590 constitutes an establishment of religion prohibited by the First Amendment to the Constitution, which is made applicable to the states by the Fourteenth Amendment. Second, the plaintiffs argue the Act violates a right to academic freedom which they say is guaranteed to students and teachers by the Free Speech Clause of the First Amendment. Third, plaintiffs allege the Act is impermissibly vague and thereby violates the Due Process Clause of the Fourteenth Amendment. . . .

The religious movement known as Fundamentalism began in nineteenth century America as part of evangelical Protestantism's response to social changes, new religious thought and Darwinism. Fundamentalists viewed these developments as attacks on the Bible and as responsible for a decline in traditional values.

The various manifestations of Fundamentalism have had a number of common characteristics, but a central premise has always been a literal interpretation of the Bible and a belief in the inerrancy of the Scriptures. Following World War I, there was again a perceived decline in traditional morality, and Fundamentalism focused on evolution as responsible for the decline. One aspect of their efforts, particularly in the South, was the promotion of statutes prohibiting the teaching of evolution in public schools. In Arkansas, this resulted in the adoption of Initiated Act I of 1929 [Arkansas's anti-evolution statute].

Between the 1920's and early 1960's, anti-evolutionary sentiment had a subtle but pervasive influence on the teaching of biology in public schools. Generally, textbooks avoided the topic of evolution and did not mention the name of Darwin. . . .

Holsted, a self-described "born again" Christian Fundamentalist, introduced [the 1981 Balanced Treatment for Creation-Science and Evolution-

Science Act] in the Arkansas Senate. He did not consult the State Department of Education, scientists, science educators or the Arkansas Attorney General. The Act was not referred to any Senate committee for hearing and was passed after only a few minutes' discussion on the Senate floor. In the House of Representatives, the bill was referred to the Education Committee which conducted a perfunctory fifteen minute hearing. No scientist testified at the hearing, nor was any representative from the State Department of Education called to testify.

[The] model act was enacted into law in Arkansas as Act 590 without amendment or modification other than minor typographical changes. ...

The State failed [in this trial] to produce any evidence which would warrant an inference or conclusion that at any point in the process anyone considered the legitimate educational value of the Act. It was simply and purely an effort to introduce the Biblical version of creation into the public school curricula. The only inference which can be drawn from these circumstances is that the Act was passed with the specific purpose by the General Assembly of advancing religion. ...

The plaintiffs raised two other issues questioning the constitutionality of the Act and, insofar as the factual findings relevant to these issues are not covered in the preceding discussion, the Court will address these issues. Additionally, the defendants raised two other issues which warrant discussion.

First, plaintiff teachers argue the Act is unconstitutionally vague to the extent that they cannot comply with its mandate of "balanced" treatment without jeopardizing their employment. The argument centers around the lack of a precise definition in the Act for the word "balanced." Several witnesses expressed opinions that the word has such meanings as equal time, equal weight, or equal legitimacy. Although the Act could have been more explicit, "balanced" is a word subject to ordinary understanding. The proof is not convincing that a teacher using a reasonably acceptable understanding of the word and making a good faith effort to comply with the Act will be in jeopardy of termination. Other portions of the Act are arguably vague, such as the "relatively recent" inception of the earth and life. The evidence establishes, however, that relatively recent means from 6,000 to 20,000 years, as commonly understood in creation science literature. . . .

The plaintiffs' other argument revolves around the alleged infringement by the defendants upon the academic freedom of teachers and students. It is contended this unprecedented intrusion in the curriculum by the State prohibits teachers from teaching what they believe should be taught or requires them to teach that which they do not believe is proper. The evidence reflects that traditionally the State Department of Education, local school boards and administration officials exercise little, if any, influence upon the subject matter taught by classroom teachers. Teachers have been given freedom to teach and emphasize those portions of subjects the individual teacher considered important. The limits to this discretion have generally been derived from the approval of textbooks by the State Department and preparation of curriculum guides by the school districts.

Several witnesses testified that academic freedom for the teacher means, in substance, that the individual teacher should be permitted unlimited discretion subject only to the bounds of professional ethics. The Court is not prepared to adopt such a broad view of academic freedom in the public schools.

In any event, if Act 590 is implemented, many teachers will be required to teach material in support of creation science which they do not consider academically sound. Many teachers will simply forego teaching subjects which might trigger the "balanced treatment" aspects of Act 590 even though they think the subjects are important to a proper presentation of a course.

Implementation of Act 590 will have serious and untoward consequences for students, particularly those planning to attend college. Evolution is the cornerstone of modern biology, and many courses in public schools contain subject matter relating to such varied topics as the age of the earth, geology and relationships among living things. Any student who is deprived of instruction as to the prevailing scientific thought on these topics will be denied a significant part of science education. Such a deprivation through the high school level would undoubtedly have an impact upon the quality of education in the State's colleges and universities, especially including the pre-professional and professional programs in the health sciences.

The defendants argue in their brief that evolution is, in effect, a religion, and that by teaching a religion which is contrary to some students' religious views, the State is infringing upon the student's free exercise rights under the First Amendment. Mr. Ellwanger's legislative findings, which were adopted as a finding of fact by the Arkansas Legislature in Act 590, provides:

> Evolution-science is contrary to the religious convictions or moral values or philosophical beliefs of many students and parents, including individuals of many different religious faiths and with diverse moral and philosophical beliefs. (Act 590, §7[d].)

The defendants argue that the teaching of evolution alone presents both a free exercise problem and an establishment problem which can only be redressed by giving balanced treatment to creation science, which is admittedly consistent with some religious beliefs. . . . The argument has no legal merit.

If creation science is, in fact, science and not religion, as the defendants claim, it is difficult to see how the teaching of such a science could "neutralize" the religious nature of evolution.

Assuming for the purposes of argument, however, that evolution is a religion or religious tenet, the remedy is to stop the teaching of evolution; not establish another religion in opposition to it. Yet it is clearly established in the case law, and perhaps also in common sense, that evolution is not a religion and that teaching evolution does not violate the Establishment Clause.

The defendants presented Dr. Larry Parker, a specialist in devising curricula for public schools. He testified that the public school's curriculum should reflect the subjects the public wants taught in schools. The witness said that polls indicated a significant majority of the American public thought creation science should be taught if evolution was taught. The point of this testimony was never placed in a legal context. No doubt a sizeable majority of Americans believe in the concept of a Creator or, at least, are not opposed to the concept and see nothing wrong with teaching school children about the idea.

The application and content of First Amendment principles are not determined by public opinion polls or by a majority vote. Whether the proponents of Act 590 constitute the majority or the minority is quite irrelevant under a constitutional system of government. No group, no matter how large or small, may use the organs of government, of which the public schools are the most conspicuous and influential, to foist its religious beliefs on others.

The Court closes this opinion with a thought expressed eloquently by the great Justice Frankfurter:

> We renew our conviction that "we have staked the very existence of our country on the faith that complete separation between the state and religion is best for the state and best

for religion." [*Everson v. Board of Education*, 330 U.S. at 59]. If nowhere else, in the relation between Church and State, "good fences make good neighbors." [*McCollum v. Board of Education*, 333 U.S. 203, 232 (1948).]

An injunction will be entered permanently prohibiting enforcement of Act 590.

It is so ordered this January 5, 1982.

--WILLIAM R. OVERTON *in United States District Court, Eastern District of Arkansas, Western Division.*

Definitions

agnostic - someone who believes that there can be no proof of the existence of God but does not deny the possibility that God exists

atheist - one who denies the existence of God

creationist - one who believes the world was created by God as described in the Bible

defense - the lawyers representing the defendant (the accused)

evolutionist - one who believes that species evolved, or developed gradually, over time through natural selection

Fundamentalist - someone who believes in the literal truth of the Bible

grand jury - a jury of 12 to 23 people formed to evaluate accusations against persons charged with crime, to decide whether there is enough evidence for an indictment

injunction - a court remedy which forbids a defendant from doing some act

polemic - a controversy or argument

prosecution - the lawyers pursuing a case for the government and the people

repeal - to revoke or void an existing law

scientific creationist - a creationist who uses science to back his beliefs

statute - a law enacted by a legislature

verdict - the decision reached by a jury at the conclusion of a trial

Notes

Biblical creation story (p. 4):   The Bible actually contains two creation stories. Both are in Genesis, which is the first book of the Old Testament. The first creation story (Gen. 1:1-2:3), referred to here, describes God creating the world in six days and resting on the seventh. The second creation story (Gen. 2:4-25) tells of the Lord God creating the earth and the heavens, and gives the story of Adam and Eve in the garden of Eden.

indict (p. 6):   Scopes had already been indicted (formally accused in writing) on May 25, 1925, but there was some question as to the validity of that indictment. To avoid any technical objections on appeal, all parties to the case agreed to seek a new indictment.

statute (p. 6):   The words *statute*, *law*, and *act* can all be used to refer to laws enacted by the legislature.

order (p. 7):   As used by biologists, *order* is the category of plants and animals ranking above the family and below the class. For example, humans belong to the class of Mammals, the order of Primates, the family of Hominidae, and the species of Homo sapiens.

bill (p. 11): A true bill is another name for an indictment. It is merely a charge, which must be proved at trial beyond a reasonable doubt before a defendant may be convicted.

Lyell (p. 13): Darwin was greatly influenced by Charles Lyell's book *Principles of Geology*. Rather than relying on great catastrophes, Lyell looked to everyday forces such as wind and water to explain how the earth's land had been shaped and sculpted.

inheritance through reproduction (p. 14): Darwin's work on natural selection predated the study of genetics. (Gregor Mendel published his paper on the principles of heredity, describing his genetic experiments with peas, in 1866; Francis Crick and James Watson discovered DNA in 1953.)

Wilson administration (p. 15): Woodrow Wilson served two terms as U.S. President, from 1913-1921.

First and *Fourteenth Amendments* (p. 42): One of the guarantees in the First Amendment to the U.S. Constitution is freedom of religion: "Congress shall make no law respecting an establishment of religion, or prohibiting the free exercise thereof . . ." The Fourteenth Amendment applies these same restrictions on governmental power to the states.

Bibliography

Ashby, LeRoy. *William Jennings Bryan: Champion of Democracy.* Boston: G.K. Hall & Co., 1987.

Asimov, Isaac. *In the Beginning: Science Faces God in The Book of Genesis.* London: New English Library, 1981.

Cherny, Robert. *A Righteous Cause: The Life of William Jennings Bryan.* Boston: Little, Brown & Co., 1985.

Darrow, Clarence. *The Story of My Life.* New York: Charles Scribner's Sons, 1932, 1960.

Darwin, Charles. *The Origin of Species.* 1859. Reprint, New York and London: W.W. Norton & Co., Inc., 1975.

Eldredge, Niles. *The Monkey Business: A Scientist Looks at Creationism.* New York: Washington Square Press, 1982.

Eve, Raymond. *The Creationist Movement in Modern America.* Boston: G.K. Hall & Co., 1991.

Johnson, Phillip. *Darwin on Trial.* Washington, D.C.: Regnery Gateway, 1991.

La Follette, Marcel C., ed. *Creationism, Science, and the Law: The Arkansas Case.* Cambridge, Ma.: MIT Press, 1984.

Larson, Edward. *Trial and Error: The American Controversy over Creation and Evolution.* New York and Oxford: Oxford University Press, 1989.

Levine, Lawrence. *Defender of the Faith: William Jennings Bryan: The Last Decade, 1915-1925.* London and New York: Oxford University Press, 1965.

Metzger, Oren and William Hilleary. *The World's Most Famous Court Trial: Tennessee Evolution Case.* Tenn.: 1925. Reprint, Rhea County Historical Society, 1978, 1990. (transcript of the Scopes Trial)

Montagu, Ashley, ed. *Science and Creationism.* Oxford and New York: Oxford University Press, 1984.

Numbers, Ronald. *The Creationists: The Evolution of Scientific Creationism.* New York: Alfred A. Knopf, Inc., 1992.

Spong, John Shelby. *Rescuing the Bible from Fundamentalism: A Bishop Rethinks the Meaning of Scripture.* New York: HarperCollins, 1991.

Stone, Irving. *Clarence Darrow For the Defense.* New York: Doubleday & Co., Inc., 1941.

Further Reading for Students

Blackmore, Vernon and Andrew Page. *Evolution: The Great Debate.* Oxford: Lion Publishing, 1989.

Gamlin, Linda. *Evolution.* London and New York: Eyewitness Science series, Dorling Kindersley, 1993.

McGowen, Tom. *The Great Monkey Trial: Science Versus Fundamentalism in America.* New York: Franklin Watts, 1990.

Scopes, John T. and James Presley. *Center of the Storm: Memoirs of John T. Scopes.* New York: Holt, Rinehart and Winston, 1967.

Skelton, Renee. *Charles Darwin and the Theory of Natural Selection.* New York: Barron's Educational Series, Inc., 1987.